RUBANK
Treasures
for ALTO SAXOPHONE

ONLINE MEDIA INCLUDED
Audio Recordings
Printable Piano Accompaniments

PLAYBACK+
Speed · Pitch · Balance · Loop

CONTENTS

To access recordings and PDF piano accompaniments, go to:
www.halleonard.com/mylibrary

4575-5814-6445-5861

ISBN 978-1-4803-5243-8

RUBANK®

HAL•LEONARD®
7777 W. BLUEMOUND RD. P.O. BOX 13819 MILWAUKEE, WI 53213

Visit Hal Leonard Online at
www.halleonard.com

Menuetto
from Divertimento No. 1

Eb Alto Saxophone

W.A. Mozart
Transcribed by H. Voxman

Allegretto

Menuetto da capo al Fine

Pavane pour une Infante Défunte

Eb Alto Saxophone

Maurice Ravel
Arranged by Harold L. Walters

00121408

American Patrol

1st E♭ Alto Saxophone (Solo)

F.W. Meacham
Arranged by Herman A. Hummel

Tempo di Marcia
Piano

American Patrol

2nd E♭ Alto Saxophone (Duet)

F.W. Meacham
Arranged by Herman A. Hummel

00121408

Sarabande and Gigue

E♭ Alto Saxophone

Arcangelo Corelli
Transcribed by H. Voxman

Ave Maria
(Ellens Gesang III, D. 839)

Eb Alto Saxophone

Franz Schubert
Arranged by Clair W. Johnson

00121408

Presto
from Suite for Alto Saxophone

Eb Alto Saxophone

Leroy Ostransky

Adoration

Eb Alto Saxophone

Felix Borowski
Arranged by Clair W. Johnson

00121408

Allegro agitato

Tempo I

Recitative and Rondino

Eb Alto Saxophone

Paul Koepke

Andante and Allegro
from Sonata in G

Eb Alto Saxophone

Benedetto Marcello
Transcribed by H. Voxman

00121408

poco rit. on repeat

Presto
from Concerto in E Minor, Op. 102

Eb Alto Saxophone

Jascha Gurewich

Non tanto adagio
from Sonata No. 5, Op. 3

Eb Alto Saxophone

Giovanni Platti
Transcribed by Richard Hervig

00121408

Slavonic Fantasy

Eb Alto Saxophone

Hans A. Heumann
Edited by H. Voxman

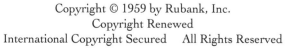

* Designates a recording "click"
(accomp. recording only)

Copyright © 1959 by Rubank, Inc.
Copyright Renewed
International Copyright Secured   All Rights Reserved

00121408

Concertino, Op. 26

Eb Alto Saxophone

C.M. von Weber
Transcribed and Edited by Henry W. Davis

★ **Foot Note:** ∽ this is a five note turn - in regular form played thus:

* Designates a recording "click" (accomp. recording only)

00121408